Papercutting
THROUGH THE YEAR

0 11557 01069 5

Papercutting
THROUGH THE YEAR

275 Patterns for Holidays and Seasonal Celebrations

Claudia Hopf

STACKPOLE
BOOKS

Published by
STACKPOLE BOOKS
5067 Ritter Road
Mechanicsburg, PA 17055
www.stackpolebooks.com

Printed in the United States of America

10 9 8 7 6 5 4 3 2 1

FIRST EDITION

Cover design by Wendy Reynolds

Library of Congress Cataloging-in-Publication Data

Hopf, Claudia, 1935–
    Papercutting through the year : 275 patterns for holidays and seasonal celebrations / Claudia Hopf. — First edition.
        p. cm.
    Includes bibliographical references and index.
    ISBN 978-0-8117-1069-5 (pbk. : alk. paper)
    1. Paper work—Patterns. 2. Holiday decorations. I. Title.
    TT870.H659 2012
    745.54—dc23
                                            2011042281

Contents

Introduction 6

New Year's Day 8

Martin Luther King Jr. Day 9

Groundhog Day 10

Abraham Lincoln's Birthday 11

Valentine's Day 12

George Washington's Birthday 24

St. Patrick's Day 25

Spring 27

April Fool's Day 34

Easter 34

Arbor Day 39

Earth Day 40

May Day 41

Mother's Day 43

Memorial Day 44

Flag Day 45

Father's Day 46

Summer 47

Independence Day 59

Ramadan 62

Labor Day 63

Autumn 64

Columbus Day 68

Halloween 69

Day of the Dead 79

Veterans Day 80

Thanksgiving 81

Hanukkah 83

Winter 84

Christmas 86

Birthday 100

Zodiac 103

Chinese Zodiac 109

Birth Month Flowers 115

Supplies and Resources 127

Introduction

This book of patterns is intended for artists, teachers, and hobbyists who want to make decorative papercuttings for the holidays. There are patterns for celebrations all through the year, for holidays from New Year's to Christmas and Hanukkah, with motifs for all four seasons, as well as zodiac signs and flowers of the twelve months for birthdays. The cuttings can be framed and used to decorate the house, applied to gifts and packages, or affixed to greeting cards.

The patterns are arranged in the book in order from January to December and include a variety for every occasion. They are all my own original designs, with some wonderful help and inspiration for ideas from my friends at the Kennebunk Free Library. There are beautiful Valentines to give to loved ones, Easter bunnies and eggs that can be added to baskets, frightful ghouls and creatures to put up for Halloween, and enchanting designs for year-end holiday gift-giving. You'll also find patterns for smaller celebrations, such as Memorial Day, Mother's Day, Father's Day, Independence Day, Thanksgiving, and just about every other holiday you can think of. There is also a wide selection of designs to reflect the mood of spring, summer, autumn, and winter.

ABOUT THE PATTERNS

In this book, you will find a nice variety of holiday and seasonal papercutting patterns. The patterns can be reduced or enlarged. The larger the design, the easier it is to cut. Smaller designs, obviously, are more intricate and challenging. The dots on the patterns indicate areas where you may punch holes with a pin.

Some of the designs lack borders. If you wish to add one, draw an outline around the design, making sure it is touching the design in several places. Then measure out about a half inch on all four sides and draw the outer line to form the complete border.

After you gain more experience, try new ideas. It can be fun to add insects or small animals to botanicals—a bumblebee to a flower, a frog under a thicket of ferns, or a chipmunk next to a tree. Doing this gives the design visual appeal and adds your own personal touch. You can use parts of patterns and add them to others if you wish.

Below are the general needs and steps for papercutting. For more complete information on the craft, including a variety of designs by other practitioners from various countries, see my book *Papercutting: Tips, Tools, and Techniques for Learning the Craft.*

TOOLS AND MATERIALS

Papercutting requires no expensive tools. Essentially, all you need is a good pair of sharp iris scissors. If you want to cut heavier papers, you will need a craft knife and a self-healing backmat. Have a pin handy, too, for punching small holes when the design calls for it.

Twenty-pound laid paper is the best type to use with iris scissors. White is preferred if you plan to stain or paint on the paper. Any paper can be used, however. You may want to experiment with magazines, calendars, rice paper, and old antique paper. You can photocopy the patterns from the book if you wish, but you may want to trace them and transfer them to paper. For tracing, you will need tracing paper, a soft lead pencil, double-sided transparent tape, and a burnishing tool or spoon.

For staining, you will need a sponge, water, instant coffee, soft tissues, and paper towels. For painting, you will need a #2 or #3 sable brush and the following watercolor paints: cadmium yellow, yellow ochre, cadmium red, alizarin crimson, Prussian blue, burnt sienna, permanent white, and lamp black. For mounting, I recommend black velour paper and an acid-free glue stick.

TRACING AND TRANSFERRING THE PATTERN

To make cuttings of the patterns in this book, you can simply photocopy them onto the paper you wish to use. If you decide to go this route, you are free to disregard this section. In some cases, however, you may not be able to load the paper you want to use into a copier, so you will have to trace the design from the book and transfer it to the paper following these steps.

Place a piece of tracing paper over the design. Be sure the tracing paper is secure by fastening double-sided tape at the top corners. Using a soft lead pencil, trace the design. Then place the tracing facedown on the paper to be cut. Secure the tracing with double-sided tape at the top corners. Rub over the lines with a burnishing tool or the edge of a spoon to transfer all the pencil lines onto the paper. Lift the tracing paper to see if all has been adequately transferred. You may need to fill in some lines.

CUTTING

Begin by cutting away the inside areas first, starting at the center and working outward. First, open the scissors slightly and poke a hole in the first center area to be cut. Keeping the scissors in place, make small snips to the edges, then cut along the line until the piece falls away. Do not tear it away. Continue in the same fashion for all the pieces to be cut out. Cut the outside edges last. This allows you to grasp the paper easier while cutting away the inside pieces.

Here are some tips for cutting.

- To avoid raised edges on the paper, hold the scissors perpendicular to the paper while cutting. This will give you a smooth cut.
- For better control, keep your cutting hand stationary while the other hand moves the paper around the blade.
- To keep from overcutting, cut on the tips of the blades, completely closing them with each cut.
- To avoid tears, always completely close the scissors before you withdraw them.
- If you find the paper is binding the scissors when you are cutting from the top surface, withdraw the scissors and cut from beneath the paper. This will help you cut easier.

FOLDED DESIGNS

This book includes a variety of folded patterns for symmetrical designs. You will need to transfer the design by tracing, so follow the steps above. To transfer, fold your paper in half and place the dotted-line side of the pattern against the fold. After the design is transferred to the paper, you will be cutting two layers.

ANTIQUING, PAINTING, AND MOUNTING

To give your cutting an antique look, lay the finished piece on a paper towel with the penciled side down. Wet a sponge with warm water and squeeze into a small dish of instant coffee crystals. The crystals will melt into a thin paste. Using the sponge, dab the paste over the cutting evenly. Remove the moisture from the cutting with a soft tissue and let it dry. Press the cutting under a flat, clear surface, such as a piece of glass. Make sure no edges are folded under. Add weight to the glass; a heavy book is handy for this purpose.

Painting the cutting is a craft in itself and something that you will develop with practice. Watercolor paints are recommended, with suggested colors listed above. First, paint the base color; then let it dry and press. Next, overlay darker shades followed by the lighter ones. Finish by painting the white highlights.

For mounting, I use black velour paper for a dramatic contrast. You may prefer a softer brown or white for background paper. Adhere the design with an acid-free glue stick. Apply a few dabs along the center back of the cutting and then press under glass.

Remember to sign and date the cutting for reference.

New Year's Day

January 1

Papercutting Through the Year

Martin Luther King Jr. Day

Birthday: January 15
Observed: Third Monday
in January

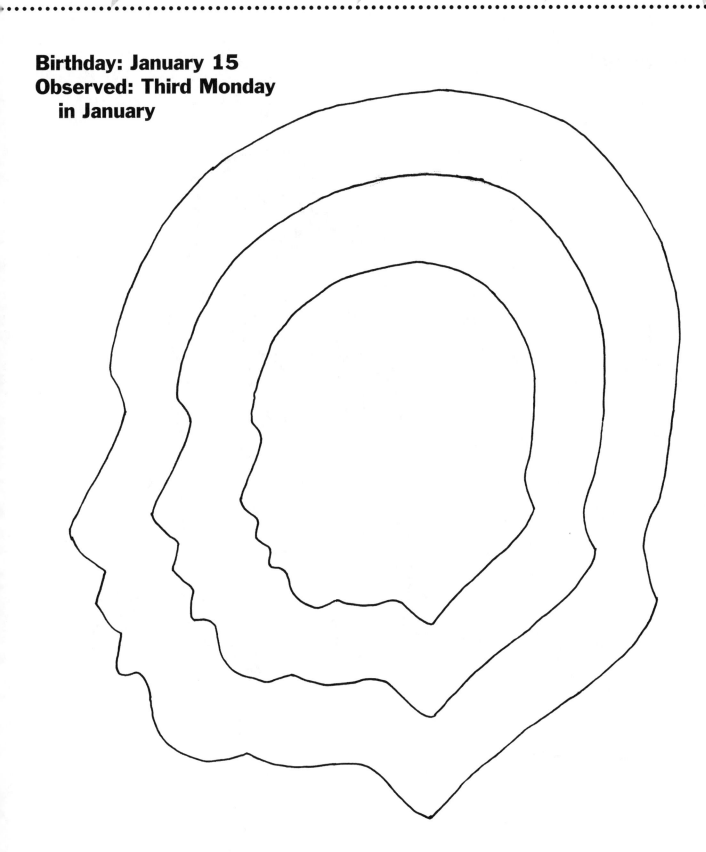

Groundhog Day

February 2

Abraham Lincoln's Birthday

February 12

Valentine's Day

February 14

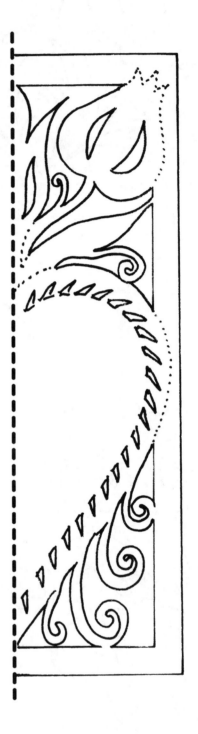

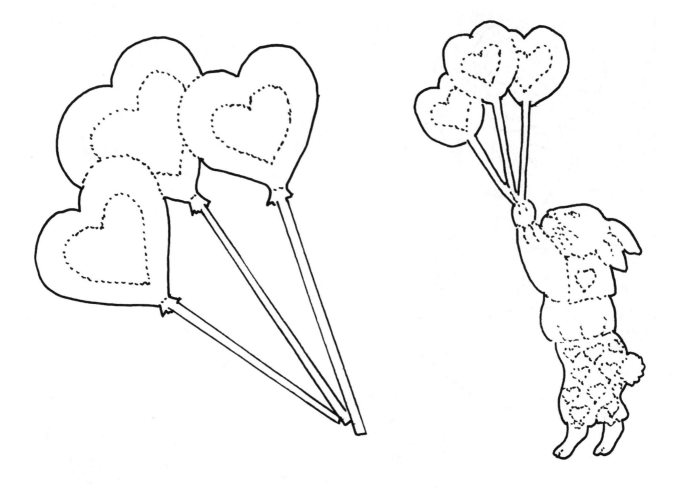

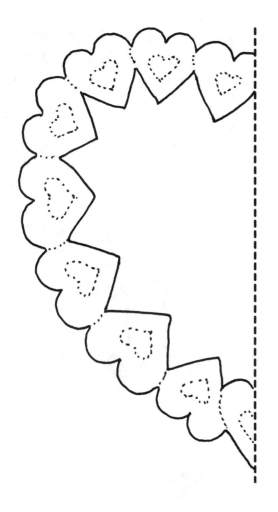

George Washington's Birthday

February 22

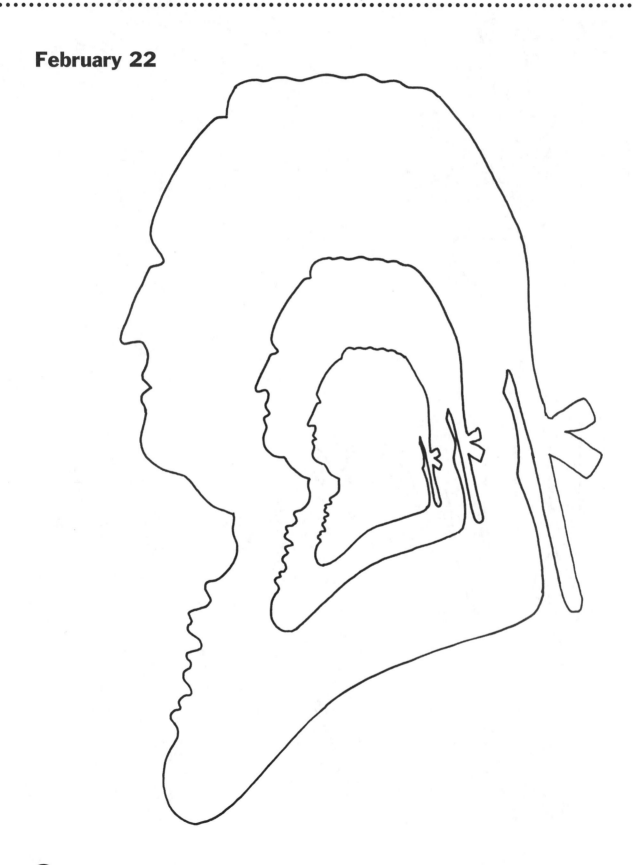

St. Patrick's Day

March 17

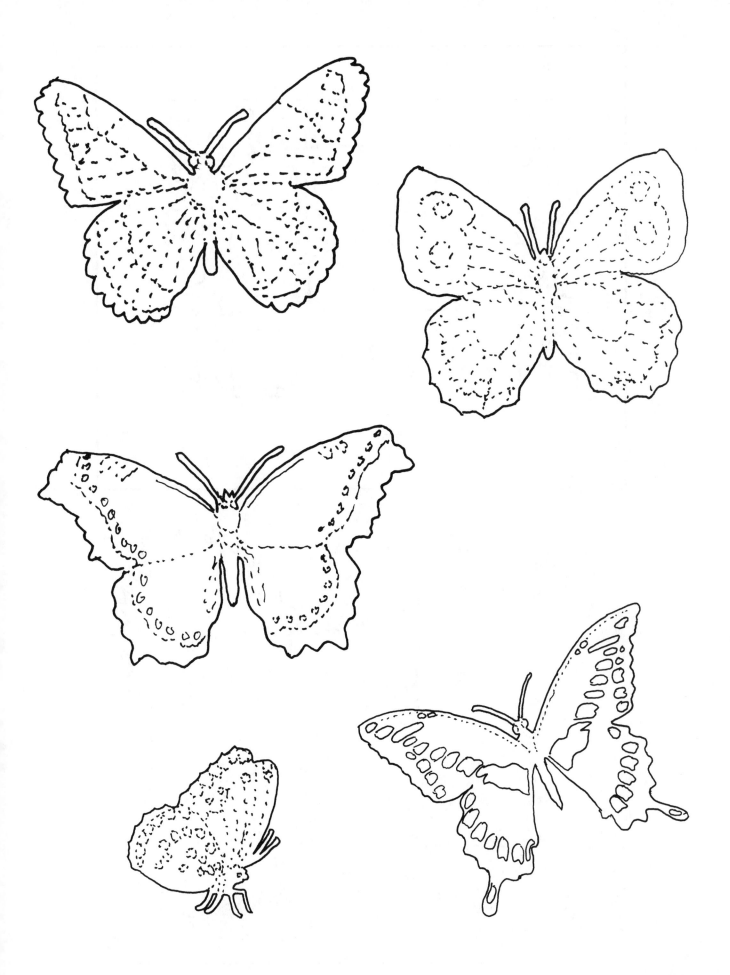

April Fool's Day

April 1

Easter

First Sunday
after the first full moon
following the first day
of spring

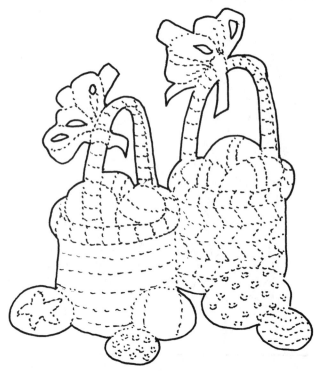

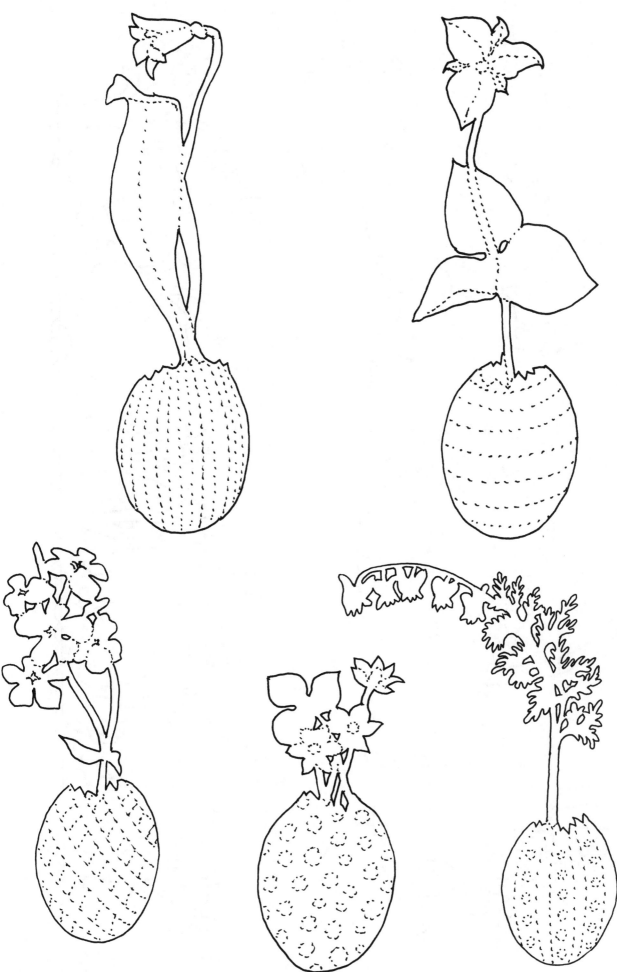

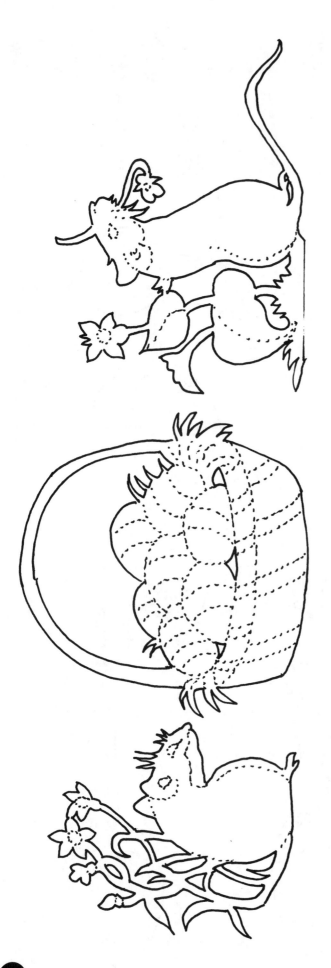

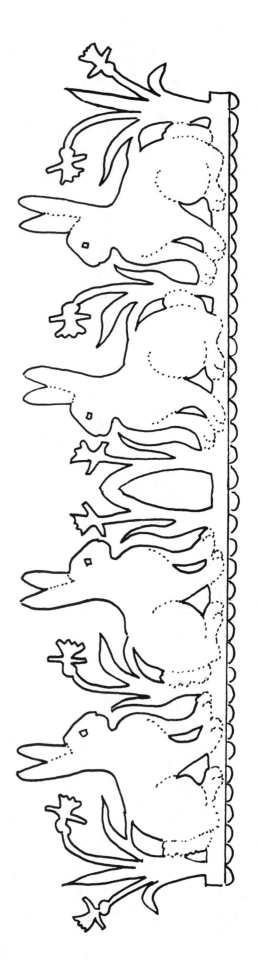

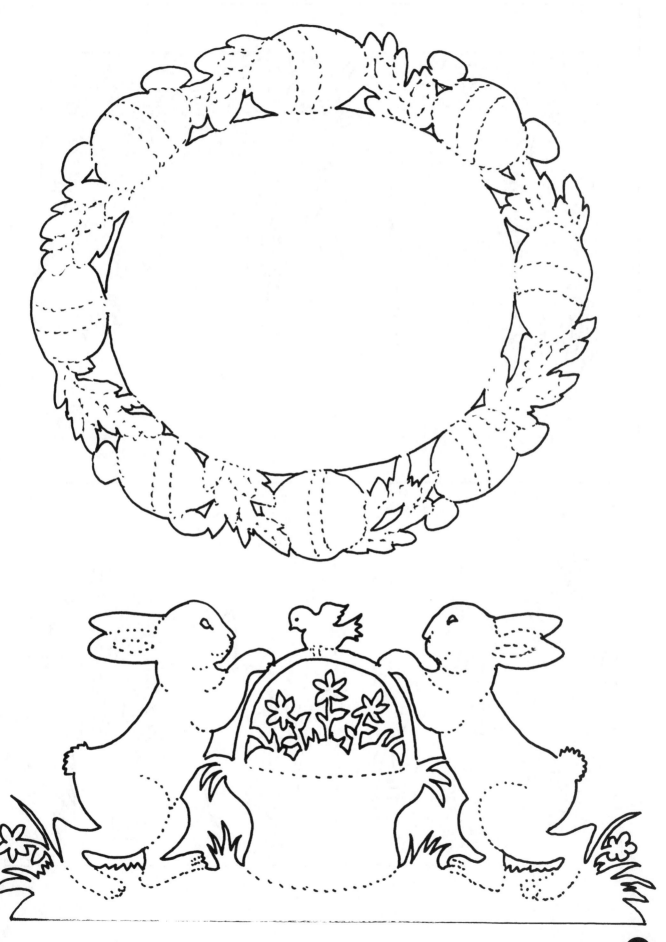

Easter

Arbor Day

Last Friday in April

Earth Day

April 22

May Day

May 1

Mother's Day

Second Sunday of May

Memorial Day

Last Monday in May

Flag Day

June 14

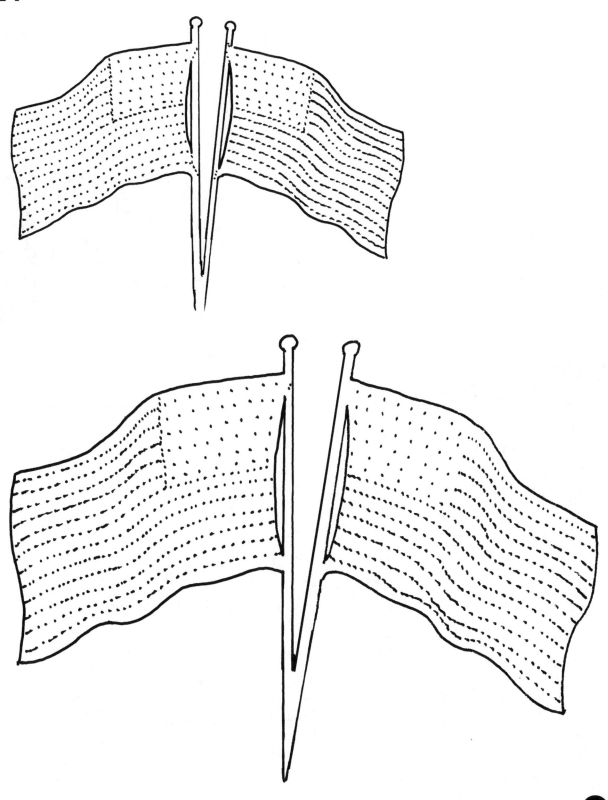

Father's Day

Third Sunday in June

Summer

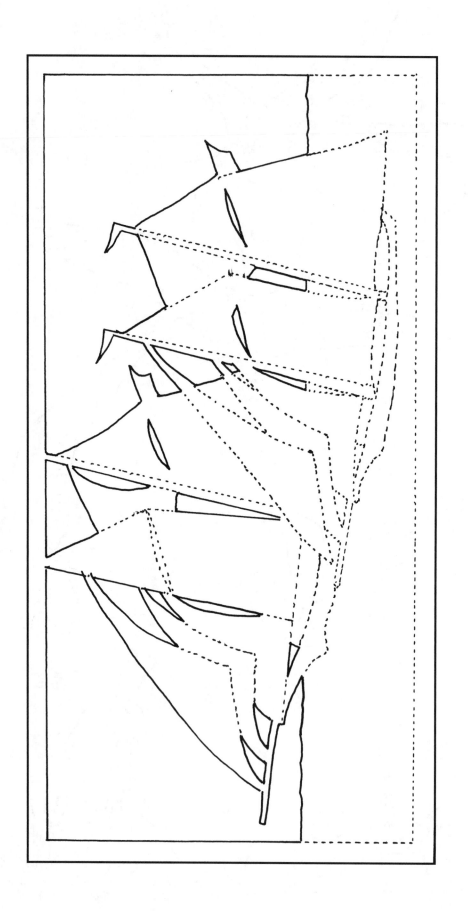

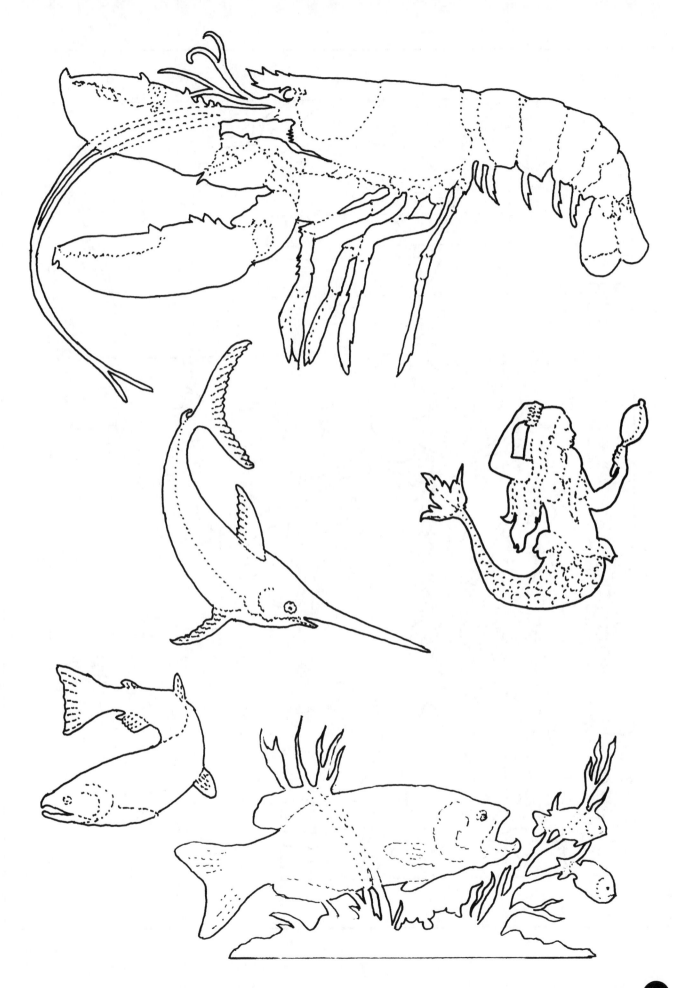

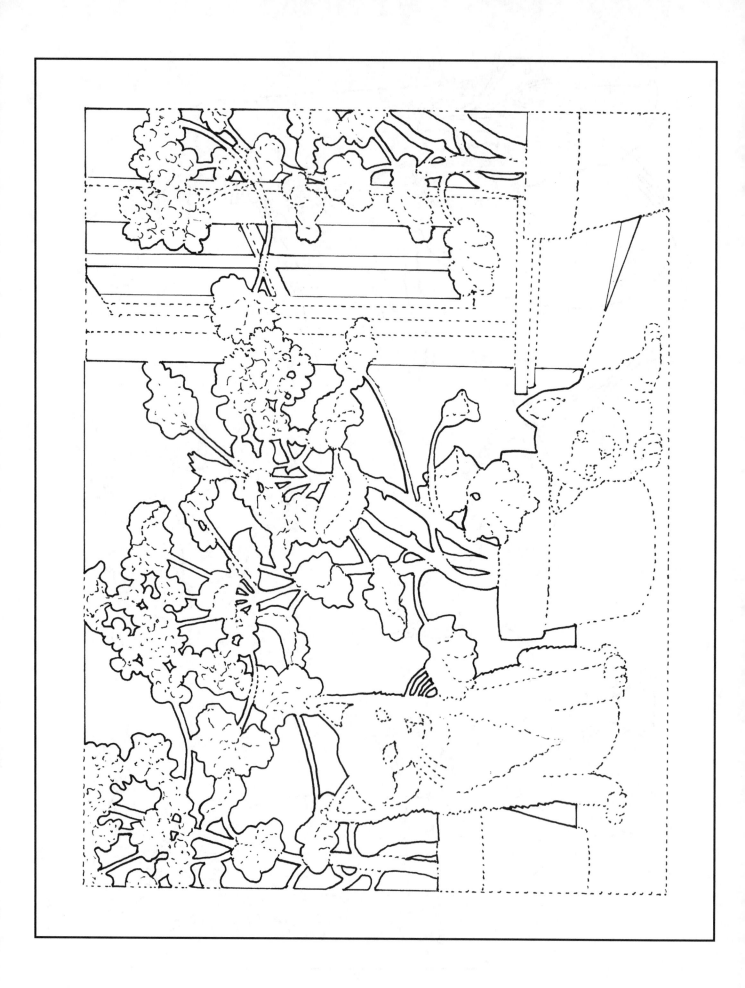

Independence Day

July 4

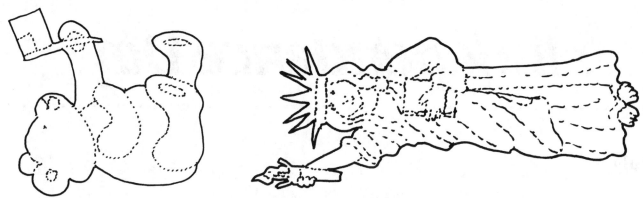

Ramadan

Month of August

Labor Day

First Monday in September

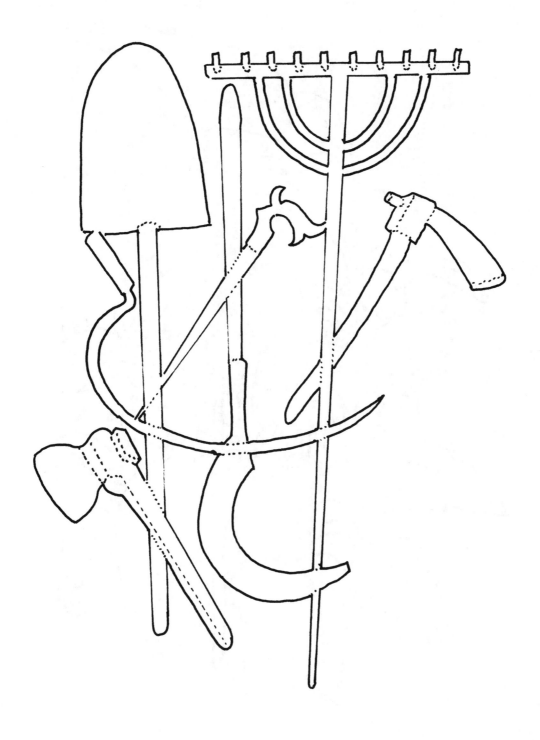

Autumn

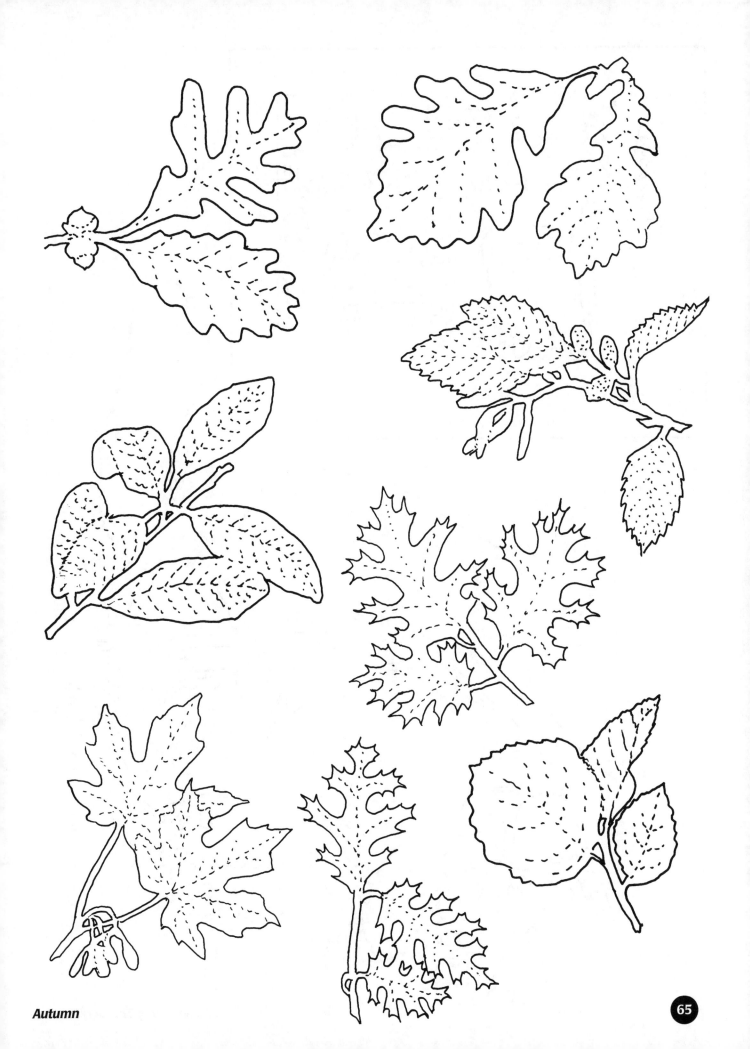

The papercut sign reads: **4 SALE**

Columbus Day

Second Monday in October

Halloween

October 31

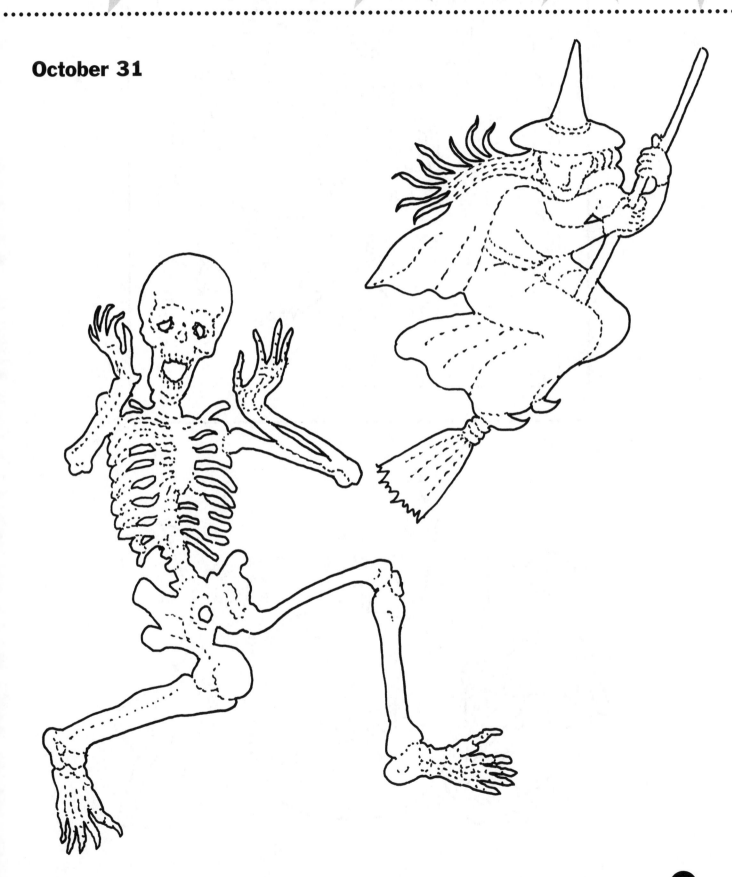

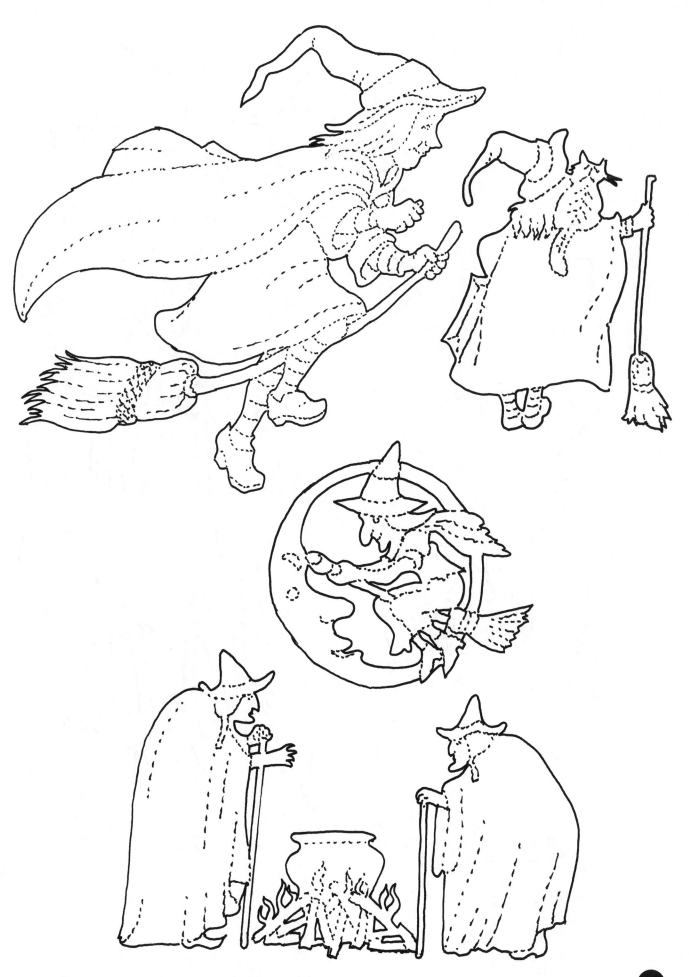

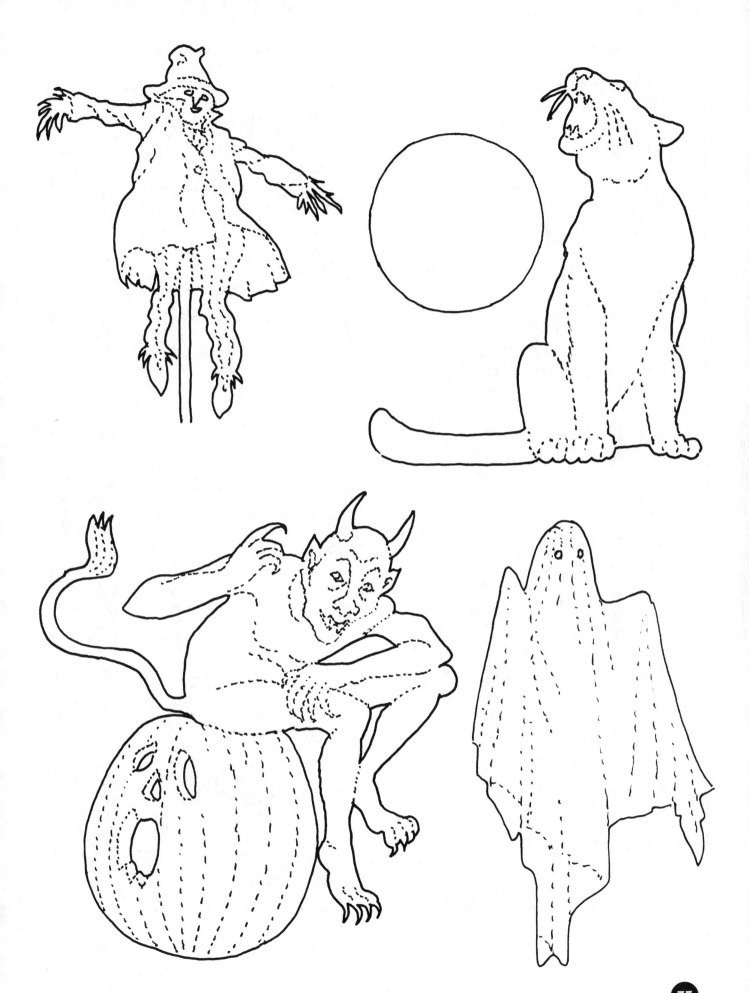

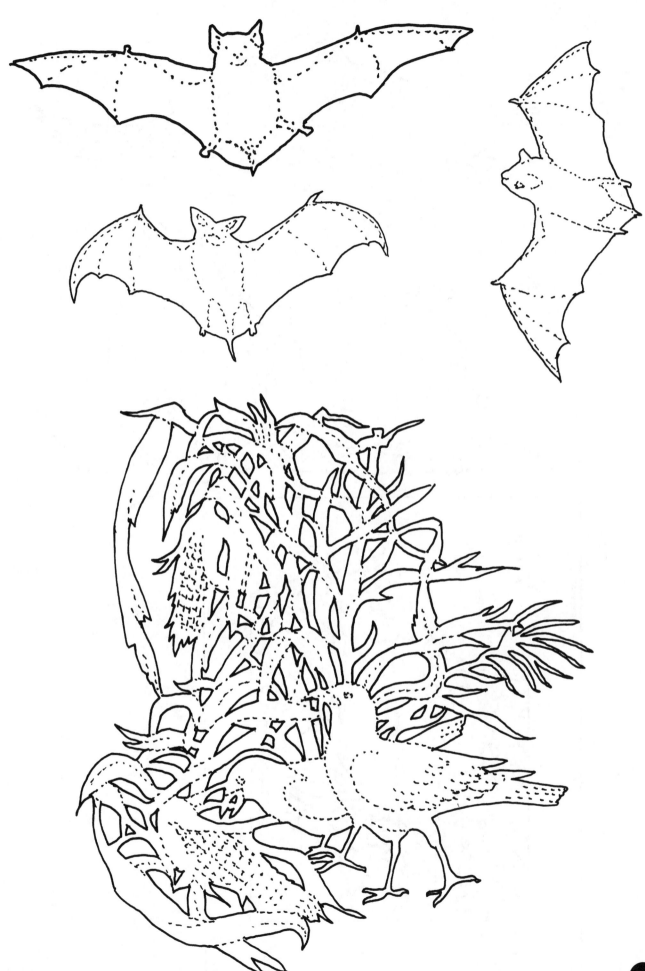

Day of the Dead

November 1–2

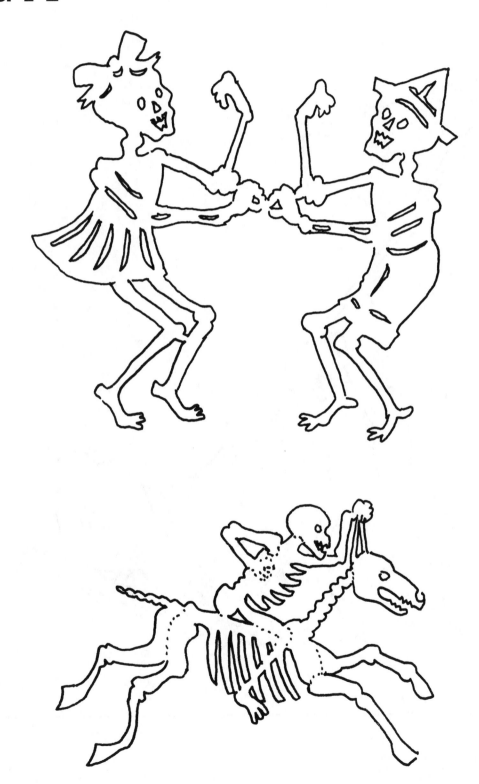

Veterans Day

November 11

Thanksgiving

Fourth Thursday in November

Hanukkah

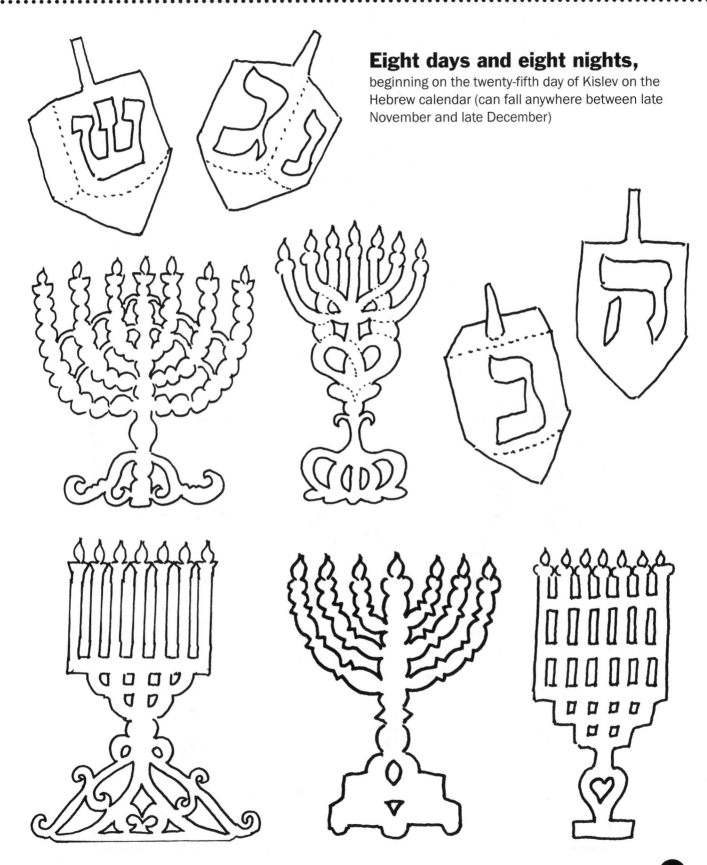

Eight days and eight nights,
beginning on the twenty-fifth day of Kislev on the Hebrew calendar (can fall anywhere between late November and late December)

Winter

Christmas

December 25

Papercutting Through the Year

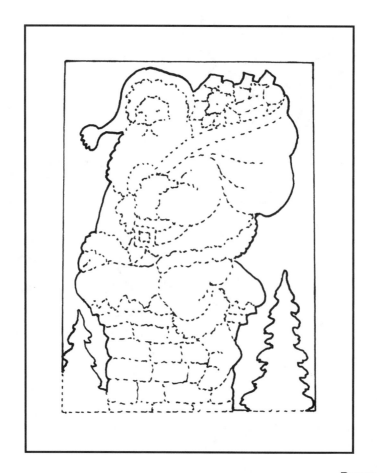

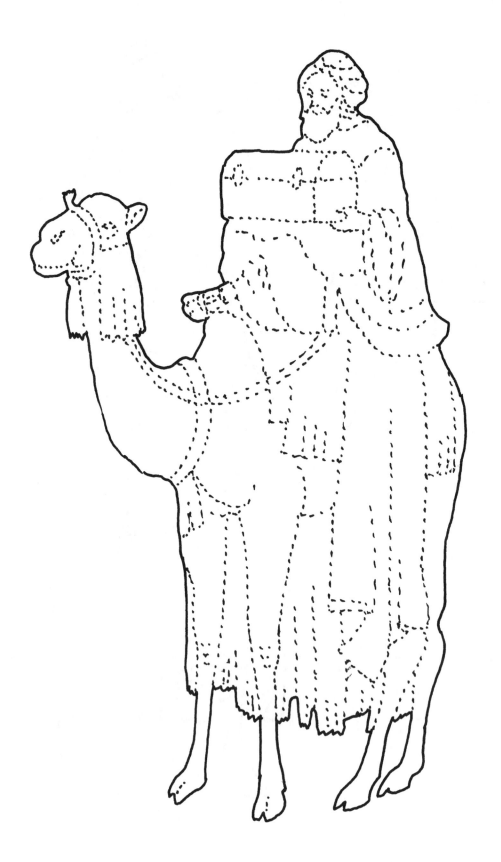

Birthday

Zodiac

AQUARIUS

January 21–February 19

PISCES

February 20–March 20

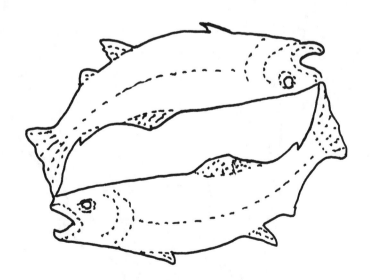

ARIES

March 21–April 19

TAURUS

April 20–May 20

GEMINI

May 21–June 20

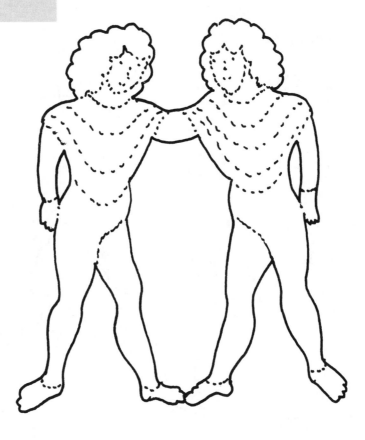

CANCER

June 21–July 21

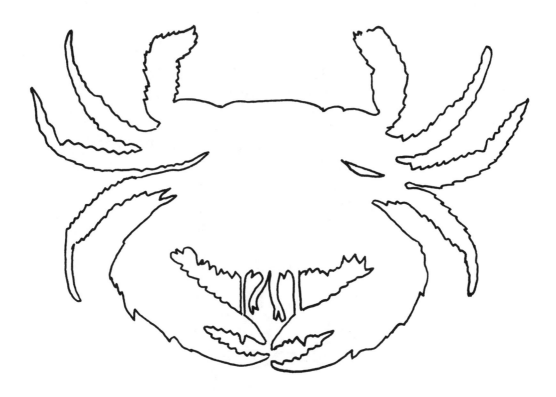

LEO

July 22–August 22

VIRGO

August 23–September 22

LIBRA

September 23–October 22

SCORPIO

October 23–November 21

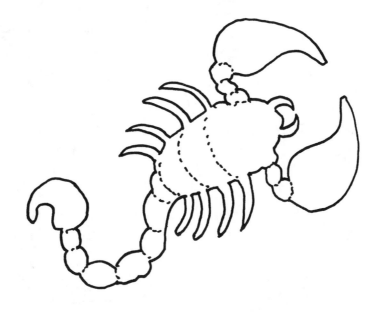

SAGITTARIUS

November 22–December 21

CAPRICORN

December 22–January 20

Papercutting Through the Year

Chinese Zodiac

YEAR OF THE DRAGON

January 23, 1928–February 9, 1929
February 8, 1940–January 26, 1941
January 27, 1952–February 13, 1953
February 13, 1964–February 1, 1965
January 31, 1976– February 17, 1977
February 17, 1988–February 5, 1989
February 5, 2000–January 23, 2001
January 23, 2012–February 9, 2013
February 10, 2024–January 28, 2025

YEAR OF THE SNAKE

February 10, 1929–January 29, 1930
January 27, 1941–February 14, 1942
February 14, 1953–February 2, 1954
February 2, 1965–January 20, 1966
February 18, 1977–February 6, 1978
February 6, 1989–26 January 26, 1990
January 24, 2001–February 11, 2002
February 10, 2013–January 30, 2014
January 29, 2025–February 16, 2026

YEAR OF THE HORSE

January 30, 1930–February 16, 1931
February 15, 1942–February 4, 1943
February 3, 1954–February 16, 1955
January 21, 1966–February 8, 1967
February 7, 1978–January 27, 1979
January 27, 1990–February 14, 1991
February 12, 2002–January 31, 2003
January 31, 2014–February 18, 2015
February 17, 2026–February 5, 2027

YEAR OF THE GOAT

February 17, 1931–February 5, 1932
February 5, 1943–January 24, 1944
January 24, 1955–February 11, 1956
February 9, 1967–January 29, 1968
January 28, 1979–February 15, 1980
February 15, 1991–February 3, 1992
February 1, 2003–January 21, 2004
February 19, 2015–February 7, 2016
February 6, 2027–January 26, 2028

YEAR OF THE MONKEY

February 6, 1932–January 25, 1933
January 25, 1944–February 12, 1945
February 12, 1956–January 30, 1957
January 30, 1968–February 16, 1969
February 16, 1980–February 4, 1981
February 4, 1992–January 22, 1993
January 22, 2004–February 8, 2005
February 8, 2016–January 27, 2017
January 26, 2028–February 12, 2029

YEAR OF THE ROOSTER

January 26, 1933–February 13, 1934
February 13, 1945–February 1, 1946
January 31, 1957–February 17, 1958
February 17, 1969–February 5, 1970
February 5, 1981–January 24, 1982
January 23, 1993–February 9, 1994
February 9, 2005–January 28, 2006
January 28, 2017–February 15, 2018
February 13, 2029–February 2, 2030

Chinese Zodiac

YEAR OF THE DOG

February 14, 1934–January 25, 1935
February 2, 1946–January 21, 1947
February 17, 1958–February 8, 1959
February 6, 1970–January 26, 1971
January 25, 1982–February 12, 1983
February 9, 1994–January 30, 1995
January 29, 2006–February 17, 2007
February 16, 2018–February 4, 2019
February 3, 2030–January 22, 2031

YEAR OF THE PIG

February 16, 1923–February 4, 1924
February 4, 1935–January 23, 1936
January 22, 1947–February 9, 1948
February 8, 1959–January 27, 1960
January 27, 1971–February 14, 1972
February 13, 1983–February 1, 1984
January 31, 1995–February 18, 1996
February 16, 2007–February 6, 2008
February 5, 2019–January 24, 2020
January 23, 2031–February 10, 2032

YEAR OF THE RAT

February 5, 1924–January 24, 1925
January 24, 1936–February 10, 1937
February 10, 1948–January 28, 1949
January 28, 1960–February 14, 1961
February 15, 1972–February 2, 1973
February 2, 1984–February 19, 1985
February 18, 1996–February 6, 1997
February 7, 2008–January 25, 2009
January 24, 2020–February 11, 2021

YEAR OF THE OX

January 25, 1925–February 12, 1926
February 11, 1937–January 30, 1938
January 29, 1949–February 16, 1950
February 15, 1961–February 4, 1962
February 3, 1973–January 22, 1974
February 20, 1985–February 8, 1986
February 7, 1997–January 28, 1998
January 26, 2009–February 14, 2010
February 12, 2021–January 31, 2022

Chinese Zodiac

YEAR OF THE TIGER

February 13, 1926–February 1, 1927
January 31, 1938–February 18, 1939
February 17, 1950–February 5, 1951
February 5, 1962–January 24, 1963
January 23, 1974–February 10, 1975
February 9, 1986–January 28, 1987
January 28, 1998–February 15, 1999
February 15, 2010–February 2, 2011
February 1, 2022–January 21, 2023

YEAR OF THE RABBIT

February 2, 1927–January 22, 1928
February 19, 1939–February 7, 1940
February 6, 1951–January 26, 1952
January 25, 1963–February 12, 1964
February 11, 1975–January 30, 1976
January 29, 1987–February 16, 1988
February 16, 1999–February 4, 2000
February 3, 2011–January 22, 2012
January 22, 2023–February 9, 2024

Birth Month Flowers

CARNATION AND SNOWDROP

January

DAFFODIL
March

SWEET PEA AND DAISY

April

LILY OF THE VALLEY

May

ROSE

June

LARKSPUR AND WATER LILY

July

GLADIOLUS AND POPPY

August

ASTER AND MORNING GLORY

September

CALENDULA AND MARIGOLD

October

CHRYSANTHEMUM

November

NARCISSUS

December

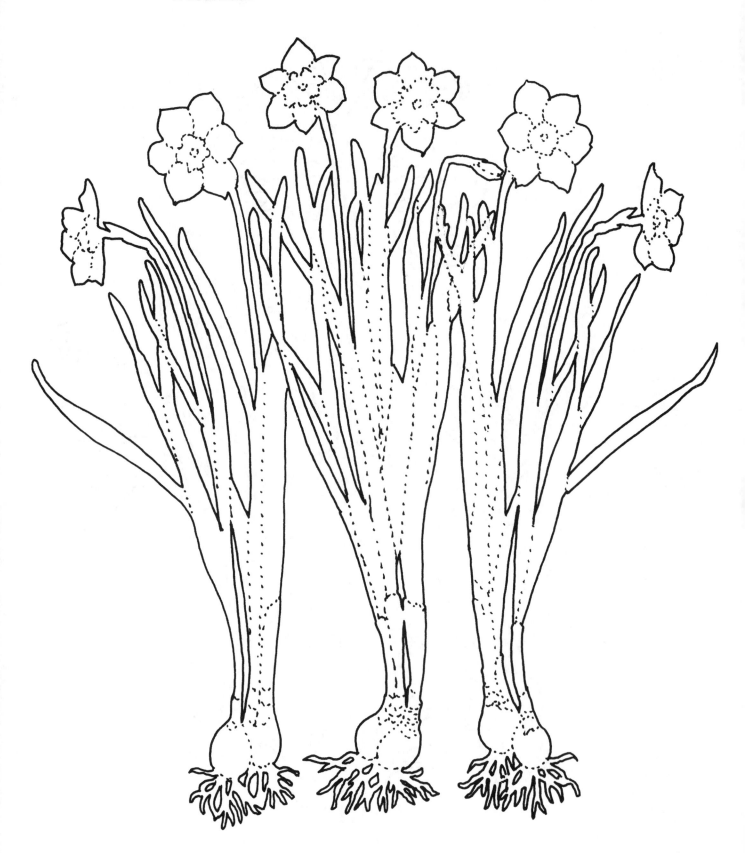

Supplies and Resources

THE GUILD OF AMERICAN PAPERCUTTERS

www.papercutters.org

This guild was established to promote the craft in North America, but includes members from Europe, Australia, and Asia. Membership ranges from beginners to full-time artists, teachers, and collectors. The guild publishes *First Cut* magazine quarterly.

PAPERCUTTINGS BY ALISON

P.O. Box 2771
Sarasota, FL 34230
(941) 378-8411
www.papercuttingsbyalison.com

Papercuttings by Alison is the creator and distributor of the largest variety of papercutting patterns and supplies. Alison Cosgrove Tanner's interest in papercutting began in 1966 when she was nine years old and her family visited the home of Hans Christian Andersen in Odense, Denmark. Andersen's papercuttings inspired Alison. She started her own business in 1984. Over the years, Alison's husband, Chuck Tanner, and her mother and father, Gloria and Don Cosgrove, have all shared in the creative art and work together in the business, supplying cutters with scissors, various papers, patterns, and books on papercutting. An annual catalog is available.

A.C. MOORE

www.acmoore.com

MICHAEL'S

www.michaels.com

SAX ARTS AND CRAFTS

P.O. Box 510710
New Berlin, WI 53151
www.saxarts.com

They offer "everything your art desires."

THE SHARPENING COMPANY

3702 West Sample Street, Suite 1105
South Bend, IN 46619
www.tsharp.com

The Sharpening Company has been in business for more than twenty-five years repairing cutting instruments. They can produce ultrasharp edges without altering the original design of the blade. Minimal metal is removed, and only as necessary.

UTRECHT ART SUPPLIES

6 Corporate Drive
Cranbury, NJ 08512
www.utrechtart.com

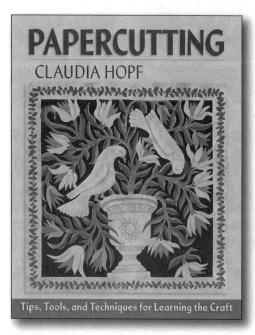